School Leadership

A Blueprint for Change

Scott D. Thomson
editor

Sponsored by the National Policy Board for Educational Administration

CORWIN PRESS, INC.
A Sage Publications Company
Newbury Park, California

For information address:

Corwin Press, Inc.
A Sage Publications Company
2455 Teller Road
Newbury Park, California 91320

SAGE Publications Ltd.
6 Bonhill Street
London EC2A 4PU
United Kingdom

SAGE Publications India Pvt. Ltd.
M-32 Market
Greater Kailash I
New Delhi 110 048 India

Printed in the United States of America

Library of Congress Cataloging-in-Publication Data

School leadership : a blueprint for change / Scott D. Thomson, editor.
p. cm.
"Sponsored by the National Policy Board for Educational Administration"
Includes bibliographical references and index.
ISBN 0-8039-6013-1
1. School management and organization — United States. 2. School administrators — Training of — United States. I. Thomson, Scott D.
LB2805.S415 1992
371.2'00973—dc20 91-32152
CIP

FIRST PRINTING, 1992

Corwin Press Production Editor: Tara S. Mead

Contents

Preface v

About the Contributors ix

1. Leadership in a World of Change
Terrence E. Deal 1

2. Leadership in Schools
Richard C. Wallace, Jr. 8

3. The Knowledge Base for School Leaders
Lloyd E. McCleary 16

4. Redesigning the Preparation of School Administrators: Toward Consensus
Patrick B. Forsyth 23

5. Professional Certification and Licensure: Governance, Organization, and Procedures
B. Dean Bowles 34

6. Strengthening Professionalism:
The Ethical Dimensions
Michael P. Thomas 46

Index 51

Preface

School leaders, like military officers in peacetime, find it difficult to become famous for the 15 minutes that Andy Warhol promised. The routines of everyday school life anesthetize public attention except when stimulated by campus crime, spectacular scandal, or a state football championship.

But the 1990s are not a peacetime for our schools. By any measure, schools are being thrust into the national spotlight, and with them school leaders. As public expectations for schools rise, as the president's six national educational goals contrast with the growing dysfunctions of classroom and family, the citizenry looks increasingly at principals and superintendents for answers. Realizing with commonsense insight that leadership makes a difference in all institutions, the public now expects leaders to make a difference in schools.

Andy Warhol's 15 minutes have arrived at the school office door, along with some high stakes. As Alvin Toffler makes clear in *Power Shift*, schools now generate the basic commodity critical to a knowledge-based economy, educated and skillful and motivated graduates. The All-American picnic is over. Schools suddenly are serious business.

What does this mean for principals and superintendents? What will they need as high-profile leaders of consensus institutions in a multiethnic, multivalue, multiexpectation society? As premium players in a suddenly high-stakes game, how do they "dress" for success? Not by adjusting a tie or scarf, but by learning new rules and applying new skills will they succeed. This requires, of course, different preparation and certification programs than typically can be found today, programs that focus on leadership skills and change processes and quality classroom instruction and problems of practice, as well as accountability for outcomes. It also requires a careful examination of the changing environment in which schools operate today.

Schools have become, in economic terms, "value-added" institutions; they increase the potential of human beings by raising their levels of thought, knowledge, skills, and socialization. The new expectations for schools, therefore, require that value added be maximized by all potential enhancements, including family involvement, community learning resources, community social services, staff development, staff involvement, technology, school learning climate, and motivation and reward systems. The integration of these enhancements will require skills that school leaders do not learn in traditional preparation programs.

As demands grow on schools for improved quality and broader services, a new leadership emerges. No longer managers of routines, school administrators need increasingly to take initiative. They must understand change as well as manage it. They must involve and motivate staff, create a positive culture, build a group vision, develop quality educational programs, provide a positive instructional environment, encourage high performance, apply evaluation processes, analyze and interpret outcomes, be accountable for results, and maximize human resources. They also must stimulate public support and engage community leaders. Finally, they must be certain that schools are persistent in getting students to understand the challenges they face, and what is required of them to compete on an equal footing in a global environment. In short, principals and superintendents must educate and lead.

All of this requires more than knowledge. It requires leadership. Most centrally, it requires effective leadership for the educational program. More than ever, school administrators are expected by the general public to ensure effective instruction.

Information increasingly drives the world economy, and it equally drives today's schools. Americans want their students to become competent in the classroom, to learn how to communicate effectively, compute accurately, think critically, show initiative in solving problems, and reflect responsible attitudes. The public has a right to expect that all students acquire these skills, and they become impatient when students fall short. Principals, especially, must provide strong leadership to improve the quality of schooling and raise student achievement to new levels. No other school official carries this responsibility so centrally, neighborhood by neighborhood, across the land.

NEW DESIGNS

What would preservice programs look like that are designed to prepare school administrators with the knowledge and skills to succeed in today's schools? What revisions are required in traditional programs?

The changes must be profound, beginning with the notion that the primary product of professional schools should be competent practitioners, and not publications. Also, the curriculum must focus on actual working environments rather than on academic disciplines, and integrate clinical exercises with class work rather than tagging it on at the end. Executive functions of the school administrator must be defined, taught, observed, and practiced by candidates rather than simply presented to them.

Educational administration is more a leadership profession rather than a technical profession, such as medicine or architecture. Principals and superintendents must achieve goals by working through others, not by the direct application of technical expertise, client by client.

A near consensus is emerging among educators, opinion leaders, and political officials that the preparation and certification of school administrators needs a major overhaul. The knowledge base has become dated and the delivery systems obsolescent. Some useful remedies are required for these middle-age afflictions.

The purpose of *School Leadership: A Blueprint for Change* is to examine the evolving nature of leadership in contemporary society and in the nation's schools, and then to propose a knowledge base and preparation and certification program that responds to these circumstances. It aims to move the conversation beyond an analysis of shortcomings to a plan for action.

Pursuing a broad perspective, the National Policy Board for Educational Administration identified six key topics critical to improving educational leadership that will move the debate forward. Invitations were then issued to authors knowledgeable in the areas selected for exploration. The requests were for focused, insightful essays rather than traditional papers.

The six statements presented in this volume represent some clear and creative thinking. They also provide the basis for further initiatives to strengthen the preparation and certification of school leaders.

RENEWING THE PROFESSION

John Gardner, founder of Common Cause and currently Haas Professor of Public Service at Stanford University, cautioned 1991 graduates about allowing their clocks to stop as they reach middle age. At a certain point in their lives, observed Gardner, some persons run out of steam. To avoid this pitfall, he recommends that people "keep curiosity, discover new things, risk, and reach out." This advice applies to professions as well. They, like individuals, need to learn and grow throughout life. In stable periods of history, meaning in the professions as well as for citizens is supplied by prescribed patterns, "a whole warehouse full of significance," according to Gardner. Today we cannot count on this heritage. Directions for developing a new professional heritage may appear unclear and confusing, but, as Irene Porter points out, if today you are not confused you are not thinking clearly.

The following six essays provide focus and useful comment for renewing the profession. With professional paralysis no longer an option, these contributions offer timely guidelines for developing leaders for the nation's new schools.

SCOTT D. THOMSON
Executive Secretary
National Policy Board for
Educational Administration

About the Contributors

B. Dean Bowles (PhD, Claremont Graduate School) is Professor of Educational Administration at the University of Wisconsin, Madison. He has served as Deputy State Superintendent of Public Instruction, member of city council, and mayor. Prior to coming to Wisconsin, he was a high school teacher and legislative advisor in California. He has been both scholar and practitioner in the field of leadership and administrator preparation. His writing includes published simulation materials and instructional cases as well as a commentary in *Education Week* entitled "Educational leadership faces a 'silent crisis'". He served as vice-chair of a legislative committee studying certification, chair of the NASSP/PSSAS Committee, member of the planning committee of the Bush Foundation Superintendents' Program Task Force, member of the Review Panel of the National Commission on the Principalship, director of Wisconsin's Task Force on Leadership and Licensure, and chair of a UW-Madison committee that revised degree and certification programs for school administrators. For 1991-1992, he will be a Fulbright Scholar to the eastern Caribbean where he will teach administration and develop preparation programs.

Terrence E. Deal (PhD, Stanford University) is Professor of Education and Human Development at Peabody College of Vanderbilt University. He serves as codirector of the National Center for Educational Leadership and Senior Research Associate at the Center for the Advanced Study of Educational Leadership. He has taught at the Harvard Graduate School of Education and the Stanford School of Education. He offers world-wide consulting services to a wide variety of organizations, including businesses, hospitals, banks, schools, religious orders, and military organizations. He has written several books and numerous articles concerning organizational issues such as change, culture management, reform, symbolism, theater, and theory. His most recent book, coauthored with Lee Bolman, is *Reframing organizations: Artistry, choice, and leadership* (1991). He also coauthored the American Bestseller, *Corporate cultures* (1982), with Allen Kennedy.

Patrick B. Forsyth (EdD, Rutgers University), executive director of the University Council for Educational Administration, is currently Associate Professor of Education Administration at The Pennsylvania State University. His research interests include the process of professionalization and the sociology of organizations. His graduate level teaching responsibilities have included organizational theory, research methods, and instructional supervision. In 1983, he was named the first recipient of the Jack A. Culbertson Award for his work in professionalization theory. He has served on the editorial boards of the *Educational Administration Quarterly, Issues in Education*, and *Educational Administration Abstracts*. Most recently, he has been active in efforts to reform administrator preparation. He chaired the national study group on reform of administrator preparation for the NPBEA and served as chief of staff for the National Commission on Excellence Administration.

Lloyd E. McCleary (EdD, University of Illinois), is professor of educational administration at the University of Utah where he has served as department chair and director of the research and development lab of the graduate school of education. He has held appointments with many schools, including the University of Illinois and the Anglican Regional Management Center, Danbury, England. He also has been a public school teacher, principal, and assistant superintendent. He was a recipient of the S. D. Shankland Fellowship and was the first recipient of the Hatch Prize for University Teaching. He led the research team of the NASSP National Principal in 1977-1978 and was a member of the research team of the 1988-1989 national study. He has chaired the National

Consortium on Field-Based Preparation, the CFK Ltd. Foundation's Principal Renewal Project, and a Task Force on Quality Staff for the Public Schools. He led a major project that developed a module-based preparation program for principals that has been used in more than 100 universities world-wide and was recognized as an exemplary program by Phi Delta Kappa. He led a similar training program for the Office of Research of the United States Army. He has directed more than 30 funded projects dealing with educational programs for such agencies as the the United States Department of Defense Dependent Schools and the Christian Children's Fund. He has served as academic specialist for the Department of State, NASSP Visiting Scholars Program, Advisor to the Office of the Queen of Jordan, and UNESCO. His scholarly writing includes eight books, and numerous articles, monographs, and research reports.

Michael P. Thomas (MS, University of Wisconsin, Madison) received his Bachelor of Arts from St. John's University in Collegeville, Minnesota with majors in Philosophy and English. He has taught English in the Menasha School District and at the University of Wisconsin, Oshkosh. After earning his PhD in Educational Administration, he joined the staff of the Coordinating Committee for Higher Education in Wisconsin and was an instructor of Philosophy of Education in the College of Education at the University of Wisconsin, Madison. In 1962, he accepted an appointment at The University of Texas, Austin. He teaches courses in Organizational Design and Ethical Issues in Educational Decision Making. He has served as Chair of the Department of Educational Administration and is currently the Chair of the Graduate Studies Committee and Graduate Advisor in that Department. He has also served as a member of the Board of Directors of the National Council of Professors of Educational Administration.

Scott D. Thomson (EdD, Stanford University) is Executive Secretary of the National Policy Board of Educational Administration. From 1974 to 1990, he served first as Deputy Executive Director, then Executive Director, of the National Association of Secondary School Principals. He has written extensively, with 46 articles published in magazines such as *Phi Delta Kappan, School Leadership, The*

School Administration, and the NASSP *Bulletin*. He has written and coauthored five monographs and one book, *Principals for our changing schools*. His latest work is a summary chapter for *Democratic leadership: The changing context of administrative preparation* to be published in December 1991. He began teaching in 1957 after serving for four years as an officer in the United States Army. He later became principal of Ellwood P. Cubberley High School in Palo Alto, California, and superintendent of the Evanston, Illinois, Township High School District. Honors include a Rotary International Foundation Fellowship to the University of Malaysia, a Stanford University Scholarship, an honorary doctorate from Bellarmine University of Louisville, and the Alumni Citation from Willamette University.

Richard C. Wallace, Jr. (EdD, Boston College) has been superintendent of Pittsburgh schools since 1980. The Teacher Centers at Schenley High School, Greenway Middle, and Brookline Elementary reflect his district's intense commitment to revitalize its teaching force. Upon graduation from Gorham, Maine, State College, Dr. Wallace began his career as a teaching principal in Maine. Between 1960 and 1966, while earning his master's and doctorate degrees, he made the transition from classroom teacher to administrator. From 1968 to 1973, he broadened his perspectives on education by taking positions in the field of educational research. After a year as a postdoctoral fellow in Educational Research at Stanford University, he served as Director of the Eastern Regional Institute for Education in Syracuse and later was Deputy Director for Program Planning and Evaluation at the Research and Development Center for Teacher Education at The University of Texas. He is a senior lecturer in Educational Administration at the University of Pittsburgh and a research associate at the University's Learning Research and Development Center. In 1990, he became the first school superintendent to receive the Harold W. McGraw, Jr., Prize in Education.

1. Leadership in a World of Change

Terrence E. Deal

In normal times, people look to managers for predictable, smooth-running, cost-effective operations. Managers help to supply the clarity, certainty, and efficiency required to get the job done right. In times of crisis, however, good management is not enough. People facing uncertainty turn to leaders for direction, confidence, and hope. Leaders encourage long-range vision, spirit, and cohesion when no one is sure about what the right job really is anymore. Leadership takes us backward or ahead to discover or rediscover why our organization exists, what it stands for, and where it might be headed. As external circumstances shift and sway, organizations seesaw between their need for management and their need for leadership. The issue is not which is better, but rather what balance is best in view of contemporary challenges.

Several years ago, a national commission formally announced a time of crisis for the American system of education. The severity of the crisis was compared to war. Since then, a series of panels and commissions has reinforced the perception that our nation's schools are in trouble. If the present situation is troublesome, future challenges and reforms loom as even more awesome. We have never been particularly successful in reshaping schools. New structures, strengthened curricula, less money, and greater diversity create even more formidable new administrative obstacles to overcome. Coupled with diminished faith that our nation's schools can ever be as good as they once were—or at least competitive with schools abroad—these problems set an ambitious agenda for the 1990s. Boom or bust will hinge on how well teachers, principals, superintendents, and citizens respond.

> All this requires more than knowledge. It requires leadership; not ordinary leadership but astute leadership. Most centrally, it requires effective leadership for the educational program. More than ever, principals [and others] are expected by the general public to ensure effective instruction. (National Commission for the Principalship, 1990, p. 11)

This new call for leadership is not confined to education. Businesses, hospitals, armies, and religious orders have also begun to realize that sound management alone will not be sufficient to respond to the organizational challenges of the 1990s. Age-old questions about leadership are being reconsidered. What is it? How is leadership different from management? Can leadership be encouraged and, if so, how? Drawing on research sponsored by the National Center for Educational Leadership, this chapter reexamines the concept of leadership and suggests some directions for preparing educational leaders equal to the issues that lie ahead.

THE ESSENCE OF LEADERSHIP

Volumes of literature written over the decades have reinforced leadership as a crucial ingredient in collective endeavors. But despite all the attention, the true essence of leadership remains mysteriously elusive. Are leaders exceptionally decisive, or do they possess personal attributes that make others more willing to accept their influence? Do leaders make a difference, or do unique circumstances create leaders? Is leadership an activity of one individual who directs followers, or is leadership a process in which several people at all levels influence a group's destiny?

Modern conceptions view leadership as a complex interaction among members of an organization, in which context rather than position usually determines who will take the lead. Despite the complexities, it is possible to distill some essential attributes of leadership, irrespective of who is at the helm. While personal behavioral attributes are often the focal point, discernible patterns reveal how leaders think about or define situations that shape and interpret leadership actions.

Bolman and Deal (1991) have synthesized the organizational literature into four distinct categories, or frames, each emphasizing a different aspect of cooperative ventures. A *human resource* frame, viewing an organization as an extended family, attends mainly to the critical link between formal goals or roles and individual needs. A *structural* frame reverses the emphasis on individuals, focusing on how an organization allocates responsibilities to well-defined positions, coordinated by authority and policy and directed toward specific goals and objectives. This approach, favoring rationality and production over caring and trust, treats the organization more as a factory than as a family.

Outside the formally drawn boundaries of authority and rationality, every organization houses interest groups that marshal power to compete for scarce resources. Realistically, these special interests often have a more profound effect on behavior than goals, rules, or legitimate commands. This imagery—the *political* frame—treats organizations as jungles, where coalitions and conflict create a constant struggle for survival and ascendancy.

A final, *symbolic* frame views organizations as tribal theater, playing to audiences within and outside formal boundaries. Expressive, rather than instrumental, concerns define what an organization means and dictate how it must appear in order to be recognized, appreciated, and supported. Needs, goals, and power are seen as less important than symbols and symbolic activity in predicting what will happen or in defining what collective life means. Cultural forms such as values, rituals, heroes and heroines, legends, myths, ceremonies, and stories create a meaningful enterprise where cohesion, commitment, and confidence are more important than caring, costs, or competition.

The four frames illuminate different needs that must be addressed for a healthy, productive organization. Each frame also defines a different administrative orientation. Frames are lenses or filters that administrators rely on in determining what is going on and how they will respond in a given situation (Bolman & Deal, 1991). Administrators who prefer a human resource orientation emphasize their role as servants or catalysts, responding to or challenging individual needs and motivations. Structurally oriented administrators emphasize their role as social architects, creating a formal arrangement of roles and relationships that tap the full range of human potential and focus attention on achieving goals and objectives. The political side of an organization keeps the administrator attuned to special interests, power alignments, and shifting issues. He or she spends considerable time building coalitions around an agenda and negotiating agreements among competing and conflicting individuals or groups. Here the administrator's role is that of an advocate or statesperson. The symbolic administrator emphasizes the importance of vision, values, and virtue, and assumes the role of prophet or poet. The chief aim is to articulate a shared, almost spiritual collective quest. Drama becomes a way of life in which the administrator orchestrates and plays a role in everyday theater.

Recent studies of administrators in business, higher education, and schools suggest that most operate primarily from either a structural or human resource orientation (Bolman & Deal, 1991). In other words, a majority of administrators are most comfortable in their human relations or authority roles. What are the consequences of these patterns of thinking and behavior? Both the structural and human resource orientations are linked significantly to these administrators' effectiveness as managers as perceived by subordinates. While a political orientation appears also to be important to an individual's effectiveness as a manager, the first two frames or orientations appear to play more significant roles. However, when effectiveness as a *leader* is judged by subordinates, the pattern almost reverses. Now symbolic and political orientations play much more dominant roles. Attention to symbols, in particular, appears to be a very significant factor in effective leadership. While concerns for people and structure are an important part of effective management, the true essence of leadership appears to be predominantly political and symbolic. Leaders operate more as negotiators and poets than as servants, catalysts, or social architects. In times of crisis, especially, effective leaders barter and build coalitions, shape and reshape symbolic forms that infuse an organization with purpose and meaning.

IMPLICATIONS FOR LEADERSHIP DEVELOPMENT

To the extent that these preliminary findings have general application, we need to rethink and probably overhaul the way we prepare educational administrators. For the most part, such training is managerial. The typical preservice curriculum is laced heavily with technical subjects such as law, finance, and management skills. Secondary attention is given to interpersonal and group dynamics, drawing heavily on social science research guided mainly by highly rational methodologies. As in business, most educational administrators are trained as managers, not as leaders. In business, for example, estimates indicate that 90% of what future business administrators receive is management training. For many budding educational administrators the percentage is probably even higher. This is not to say that management training is unimportant, but at a time when most constituencies are calling for more leadership in education, our efforts to prepare such people are probably barking up the wrong pedestal.

What is the alternative? A look at innovative business and health care organizations suggests some possibilities. In a study of successful general managers in the business world, for example, Kotter (1982) finds that very early in their careers these top performers were given challenging assignments across a wide variety of functions within the same company. They learned leadership lessons from their experiences (from their failures more than their successes) and from mentors (poor examples as well as good ones). They developed a well-grounded, global sense of the business, in relationship both to the customers and to the society at large. These results support a long-standing wisdom that leadership is learned best from the school of hard knocks.

Other businesses believe that leadership can be encouraged through forward-looking development programs. The curriculum of American Medical International's (AMI) Corporation College, for example, included philosophy, the psychology of color, the game of tennis, museum curatorship, visionary leadership, and symbolism. AMI believed that individuals well grounded in the ethical, aesthetic, and liberal arts could make the best contribution to the company's leadership capital.

There are other examples of innovative approaches to leadership development, all suggesting a radical shift in how we might style education's future leadership pool. If leaders learn best from experience, then we need to provide challenging assignments early in administrative careers. Internships and practica as currently designed typically offer little besides hands-on chances to master bureaucratic and administrative minutiae. Rarely are promising candidates given significant responsibility and the opportunity to feel the awesome weight of being in charge. Seldom do they learn to give and take with political forces, or come to know where symbolic opportunities to influence events lie in the midst of the ambiguity and complexity of everyday life. Mentoring novice principals (or those in other first-time line positions) is probably more effective and also more rewarding to seasoned veterans than trying to make work for part-time interns or practicum participants.

Once young administrators have tested the limits and liabilities (as well as the promises) of being in charge, they should be ready for formal opportunities to reflect on their experiences. But the content and emphasis of their education should be shifted from technical training and the traditional social sciences steeped heavily in the scientific method to incorporate a thorough grounding in political strategy, anthropology, history, literature, philosophy, poetry, art, music, and the humanities. In addition, the process of learning would need to move from lecture and recall to case studies, films, simulations, and other approaches designed to distill wisdom from practice. By bouncing their personal experiences against collective experience and the wisdom of the ages, aspiring young administrators should develop self-knowledge, a deep understanding of the political and symbolic aspects of the context in which they will work, and a broad understanding of the past, present, and future social and economic forces that have shaped, and will shape, their institutions over time.

If we were to take these general guidelines seriously, we would have to transform completely most existing administrative preparation programs. How all this would happen—or whether it even could—is unclear. But in trying to reshape administrative preparation programs to focus on the political and symbolic aspects of administrative work, perhaps instructors of higher education could themselves take a leadership role. It is hard to prepare future leaders in contexts that are often poorly managed, overly rational, and underled.

In trying to reshape leadership development programs, it is important not to lose sight of management training or the development of managerial skills. However, at this juncture in American education, it is probably more important to have some creative leaders who are willing to take risks, and even fail, than to continue to rely too much on managers who keep trying—without success—to make a jungle or theater work like a family or a factory.

REFERENCES

Bolman, L. G., & Deal, T. E. (1991). *Reframing organizations: Artistry and choice in management.* San Francisco: Jossey-Bass.

Kotter, J. P. (1982). *The general managers.* New York: Free Press.

National Commission for the Principalship. (1990). *Principals for our changing schools: Preparation and certification.* Fairfax, VA: Author.

2. Leadership in Schools

Richard C. Wallace, Jr.

The leadership role in public schools is assuming a new dimension caused by national and international forces influencing our educational system. The public now expects educational leaders to improve the quality of schooling significantly. These presumptions require leaders first to clarify educational outcomes and assessment strategies. They also require leaders to be proficient in staff development practices, experts in labor relations, and conveners of business, political, and social service executives. The circumstances within which school leaders must function in the 1990s and beyond, therefore, dictate major changes in preparation programs.

Student achievement in the United States compares unfavorably with outcomes in Asia and Europe, according to international data. These results raise questions about the economic competitiveness of our nation in the twenty-first century unless future generations of pupils are educated more effectively than reported by present indicators. Furthermore, the changing demographics of the United States suggest that this nation must do a better job of educating an expanding population of poor and minority students. Reports indicate that these pupils are underserved by the public schools, yet these same students will form a major portion of the work force in the next century. Comprehensive, multicultural education programs will be required to motivate poor and minority students to achieve at a higher level than is typically found today. For these reasons, school leaders must exhibit a higher level of educational, civic, and political leadership than has typically been required to ensure that American citizens are prepared to participate effectively in the world economy of the twenty-first century.

Citizens, business leaders, parents, and local, state, and federal government officials are demanding a more effective American schoolhouse. Administrators at the school and district levels, therefore, must provide dynamic educational leadership to improve the quality of schooling and raise the level of student achievement. While the competent management of schools continues to be essential, a more dynamic form of educational, civic, and political leadership is required today if schools are to meet the educational challenges ahead for our nation.

ESSENTIAL CHARACTERISTICS OF EDUCATIONAL LEADERS

Educational Leadership

Perhaps the most significant recent change in educational administration is a requirement for aggressive and effective leadership at the building and the district levels. More than ever, school administrators are expected by the general public to be active leaders of the instructional program. The general public now anticipates that all pupils will master the tools of learning and apply those skills for knowledge acquisition.

Pupils must also develop the skills and habits they need to become lifelong learners; they must acquire the capability to seek out and solve academic and interpersonal problems. The broad community wants students to emerge from basic education with the competence to communicate effectively, compute accurately, and think critically. Additionally, the public wants students to possess sufficient knowledge to become effective participants in our democratic society and the world community. The business world also expects that graduates should be able to work effectively in groups and to solve the human relationship and systems problems that frequently arise in the workplace. To fulfill these expectations, educational leaders must envision strengthened schools and be able to energize professionals and the community to bring about the conditions that will ensure a high-quality educational product. They also must be capable of conveying symbolic meaning to nourish aspirations and achieve these goals.

Educational Outcomes

Effective educational leaders possess the capacity to articulate to various constituencies their vision of educational processes and outcomes. To do this, an educational leader must possess a sound and well-integrated set of beliefs about what constitutes effective teaching and learning. He or she must be able to express those beliefs by describing specific actions in which instructors and learners engage during the learning process. These beliefs must also be articulated as they relate to the outcomes of the learning process.

A successful leader must express clearly the behavioral outcomes or products that students should demonstrate at various stages in their progress toward graduation. This will allow verification of the acquired skills and knowledge that constitute the vision of quality education articulated by the leader.

As student outcomes are developed, defined, and evaluated by the school, leaders must negotiate among faculty interests to find common ground and to generate group commitment.

Educational Assessment

Concomitant with the ability to articulate an integrated set of beliefs, values, and processes related to learning outcomes, the educational leader must be able to use assessment procedures. Effective leaders communicate to teachers, learners, parents, and the general public what students have learned, specifically and without equivocation. For too long, educators in this nation have depended on a narrow set of standardized test scores as the sole criterion to judge the quality of schooling. These measures are inadequate.

More diversified sets of measures must be developed to verify student attainment of knowledge, skills, habits, and attitudes. Educational indicators must be developed and used to communicate the holistic outcomes of the educational process. These results must go beyond the traditional and narrow cognitive assessments that make up the typical product of standardized, multiple-choice achievement tests. Affective perspectives about learning by students and measures of the quality of life in schools must also be reported to parents and the public.

The educational leader of the future, therefore, must be skilled in the use of various measures that provide indicators of the "health" and productivity of a school or district. In addition, the leader must be able to communicate accurately the achievement of individual students and the meaning of this achievement to students and the broader society.

School leaders of the future must monitor a variety of indicators reflecting progress and outcomes. Included in this analysis are individual schools, pupils individually and in groups, and the district as a whole. These data demonstrate progress toward the multiple outcomes found in the vision of quality education for a district. Such leaders must be able to analyze data effectively and search for trends in a variety of educational data. They must know how and when to intervene in schools to allocate resources and take corrective actions to improve the quality of outcomes. In sum, a sophistication in seeking out and using data to inform the decision-making process is required of school leaders. They must continually scan data to measure the pulse of the community and to provide effective educational leadership.

Leadership in Professional Development

Perhaps the most important function the educational leader performs is to promote and sustain the continuing development of the professional staff. Teachers and administrators grow in technical and social competence when leaders provide a supportive climate and multiple opportunities for such growth. School leaders must develop and implement comprehensive, sequential, and long-term staff development programs to ensure that these professionals maximize their potential. They also must communicate to boards, parents, and the general public a need to support the continuing professional development of teachers and administrators. Such expenditures are necessary investments to ensure that schools and districts attain a top return on the dollar for teacher and administrator salaries. These monies for professional development promote and sustain quality education. Effective educational leaders are able to articulate this position to their various constituencies, and to link the goals of the school with the professional, interpersonal, and symbolic needs of teachers and administrators.

Civic and Political Leadership

Educational administrators need to expand their civic and political leadership in the coming decades to rally support from the lay community to improve the quality of schooling. Now, more than ever in our nation's history, American businesses recognize that it is in their own best interests to join with school leaders to pursue the improvement of public education. This action is necessary to provide current and future generations of workers for U.S. business and industry. The lack of an effective work force for the twenty-first century could result in a significant decrease in the quality of life in the United States, and a parallel decline in our international influence.

The broad international and social context within which schools already operate requires leaders knowledgeable about economic and political affairs. It also requires a perspective that incorporates schools and communities as partners. Formidable communication skills will thus be a particularly valuable asset of the new school leader.

School, Community, and Business Partnerships

Private sector partnerships can form the cornerstone of improved educational practice. Schools must open their doors to engage the community in delivering quality educational programs. Students should understand relationships between school and the workplace; schools must provide relevant career educational connections and experiences for students. School leaders who use the broad human and material resources of their communities creatively will provide lively educational experiences for their pupils.

Effective school leaders will seek the involvement of business leaders aggressively, so that the business community will support and help deliver educational programming. This interface will produce two important results. First, the business community and the schools will gain more respect for and trust in one another. Second, the pupils will experience more lively and relevant educational programs. Everyone will win.

Social Service Imperatives

In addition to civic and political leadership, educational administrators must also forge effective collaborative working relationships with the social service organizations that provide assistance to children, youth, and their families. The decline of the family as a stable institution has produced a generation of children and youth who manifest intense personal and social ills, more than can be found historically in the nation's schools. These growing problems arise from the high incidence of single-parent families, "children having children," and children born of drug-addicted mothers. Our public schools must accept children and youth who require multiple social services to be educated. The schools should provide leadership for coordinating community resources so that pupils will be provided with the services they and their families require. These difficult conditions require aggressive school leadership to form comprehensive youth services collaborations. Schools, governments, and social service agencies must plan and work together to ensure the effective delivery of all needed services that promote the educability of children and youth.

Financing Education

In the years ahead, financing public education will emerge as one of the nation's most significant issues. School leaders must underline the necessity of adequate funds for public education, and they must convince the general public and local, state, and national legislators of the wisdom of supporting public education. Citizens will need to be reminded continuously that public education has made this nation great and has produced an effective work force, resulting in a high standard of living. Educational leaders must forge and maintain coalitions of citizens, business executives, and legislators to achieve adequate financing of public education. This diversion of civic and political leadership will take on greater importance as the decade of the 1990s unfolds, and its success will depend on successful coalition building and symbolic meaning as well as the usual facts and figures.

Leadership in Labor Relations

School executives must develop good working relations with all employee groups, engaging teachers and administrators in shared and site-based decision making. This requires leaders who have a working knowledge of organizational development principles and practice; it also requires a knowledge of and the ability to apply educational change processes. Fellow professionals must be engaged in dynamic interchanges about educational and organizational matters that stretch each other's limits of creativity to produce viable problem-seeking and problem-solving institutions.

All school workers must be empowered to participate in school improvement. Clerks, custodians, cafeteria workers, and others can all be involved in promoting the quality of the workplace and the quality of schooling for children and youth. The effective school leader finds ways to involve all employees in promoting pride in the schools, and engages them in activities that bring about real changes and add symbolic meaning to their lives.

Expectations for Preparing School Leaders

New expectations for school leaders require rethinking preparation programs. Effective programs will emphasize vision building, program development, evaluation of outcomes, the ability to use multiple sources of data for decision making, and management of change. Additionally, knowledge of professional and organizational development and strong interpersonal and communication skills are critical components, because new leaders must motivate people and institutions to be dynamically interactive, professionally effective, and mission oriented.

School leaders must also be prepared for active community leadership and must possess the skills to elicit support from the business community, civic organizations, the media, and parents.

Finally, the knowledge base and skills for the new educational leadership must be grounded in sound management theory and practice so that the processes and techniques by which the missions of the school are accomplished are effective as well as efficient, allowing the educational program to be realized and students to be served.

SUMMARY

The role of the leader in public education for the 1990s and beyond encompasses educational, civic, and political dimensions. Educational leaders must articulate a coherent vision as well as define the components of quality education for students. They must motivate professionals at the school and district levels to implement that vision, while also becoming committed to and involved with a comprehensive and sustained program of staff development activities. Educational leaders must be sophisticated in the knowledge and use of assessment techniques to monitor and verify the attainment of educational outcomes at the school and district levels. And they must invoke symbolism as well as exhibit professional skill during this process.

As civic leaders, educational administrators must articulate the needs of the school and the district to several constituencies: the general public, taxpayers, business leaders, the media, and government agencies. More important, they will need to mobilize support from these constituencies to provide adequate funding for public education. Developing collaborative relationships with the business community to promote its direct involvement is one imperative for educational administrators. Another is the capacity to adjudicate the interests of various constituencies.

Finally, school leaders must be able to promote the establishment of comprehensive collaboratives that integrate the variety of social and medical services needed by children, youth, and their families. Such mobilization of community forces to promote and support public education characterizes the dynamic type of leadership required if public education is to thrive in the twenty-first century.

3. The Knowledge Base for School Leaders

Lloyd E. McCleary

Knowledge for the educational leader is analogous to the tools of the artisan. The type and nature of knowledge and its use determine the capabilities of the leader, just as the tools and talents of the artisan determine the quality of the art. The rapid expansion of knowledge and, perhaps more important, the changing conditions to which knowledge must be applied mean that knowledge for the educational leader must be more like Hemingway's "movable feast" than a smorgasbord. In this sense the knowledge base must be selective and organized; it cannot be set out merely as anything and everything that somehow might be attractive. Previous authors have treated the nature and role of school leadership. The questions addressed here are as follows:

(1) What requirements must be placed on the sources of knowledge so that educators can obtain the tools of the true artisan leader?

(2) What rubrics can be used to avoid the smorgasbord approach to the organization of the knowledge base?

(3) What is the appropriate knowledge base for educational leadership?

To lead effectively, principals and superintendents must solve problems, resolve issues, and increase individual and organizational performance at the same time they clarify, and often challenge, deeply held values and beliefs about their role in serving educational purposes. Educational leaders must possess knowledge of the potentials education has for the configuration of students being served and knowledge of the culture of schools as institutions.

Educational leaders must also possess the knowledge and skills prerequisite to the achievement of a unit of purpose and a high level of commitment from their communities and from the staffs and students they serve. This requires that educational leaders have not only conceptual and technical knowledge about education but also knowledge of social and political processes. Educational leadership is exercised through interactions with others, often involving matters of principle and personality about fundamental ideas and values of the society. Thus knowledge needed to exercise leadership also has a moral dimension.

The possession of knowledge about the topics noted above does not ensure that an educational leader will be effective. The leader must understand the *nature* and *uses* of knowledge appropriate to a given set of circumstances. This is a form of knowledge in itself and can be learned. Some situations arise that call for immediate action and prompt intervention; some are cyclical and managerial and are amenable to technical solutions and objective problem-solving methods; others are chronic, endemic difficulties that require the application of strategies, over time, to change conditions and move an organization ahead. The educational leader needs to know the differences among these, what knowledge is required and how to access it through him- or herself and others, the adequacy of the concepts from the knowledge base, and how and when to apply them.

NATURE OF THE KNOWLEDGE BASE

Agreement does exist that educational administration has a body of knowledge and is a legitimate field of inquiry. Its focus of study centers on educational problems and issues and on educational institutions. It is not unique among applied fields in that it draws on supporting disciplines, where appropriate, for concepts and methodological tools. In pursuing its scholarship it has both developed and adapted views of practice and the study of practice that have become widely shared.

Educational administration has at least four sources of knowledge:

(1) *What everyone knows:* These are the generally accepted tenets and ideals of the profession, derived from the experience of practitioners and observers of education and administrative practice.
(2) *What practice demonstrates:* These are the accounts of practices that have been shown to produce certain effects, usually through concerted efforts made to solve an important problem.
(3) *What authorities say:* These are observations, often expressed as generalizations or principles, made by those whose status, owing to experience and the quality of their scholarly study, is given special credence.
(4) *What research confirms:* These are, simply put, findings that have been confirmed by evidence, arrived at through known procedures, and subjected to critical review and further testing.

The linkages among these sources, however, are weak and need to be drastically improved. However, it must be recognized that, with rapidly changing conditions, the knowledge base will never be complete or adequate. Educational leaders must continue to be critical of the knowledge base and become more active in developing the fund of knowledge that supports their work. The competence displayed in skillful practice is both a starting point for knowledge and a test of the adequacy of the knowledge already employed.

The National Commission for the Principalship (1990) identifies two leadership dimensions. The first is a broad, encompassing leadership that influences a school's culture by creating a vision of the possible and the encouragement, innovation, and support to reach improvement. The second is a functional leadership that supplies the technical competence to "make things happen." Concerning the first dimension, the knowledge base can contribute substantive content that has relevance to all other areas. These are inquiry and ethics. *Inquiry* refers to the conceptual and technical capabilities involved in problem solving and change. School administrators need to be leaders of inquiry into the problems faced by schools and of the processes by which inquiry guides and monitors change in schooling. Inquiry includes both knowledge and reflection about needs and priorities, potentials and possibilities, and the capacity to involve others in orderly steps to improvement.

The importance of ethics and the moral questions that involve administrative relationships and policy-making have been noted. Along with these two areas are five others: schools as institutions, educational programs and instruction, organization and organizational management, school governance and external relations, and related fields. The first four conform to the performance domains of the principalship as identified by the National Policy Board for Educational Administration.

SCHOOLS AS INSTITUTIONS

School leaders need to have a perspective on the potential and profitable directions for schools and schooling. This entails a sound understanding of how schools and schooling came to be as they are and where they can make a difference in the lives of children and youth. Leaders must have knowledge of local, state, and national initiatives that have shaped the schools and their programs over time in order to formulate perspectives about the future. The social, cultural, and economic forces that gave impetus to such initiatives provide an understanding of the cultural values and the social and economic conditions for which educational solutions were sought. With this knowledge, educational leaders can better understand persistent problems and issues, trace their impacts upon local conditions, and identify trends to be monitored. The concepts essential to such understanding are contained in professional knowledge relating to education policy and change, but also in the related fields of sociology, history, and political science.

EDUCATIONAL PROGRAMS AND INSTRUCTION

The essence of education is found in school programs, curriculum and instruction, and student services. A prime component of educational leaders is the ability to conceptualize, present, and defend the educational programs for which they are responsible. This may be the one responsibility that cannot be delegated, although teachers, counselors, students, specialists, citizens, and policymakers may be involved. Program design, curriculum content selection, and instructional specifications may be executed by others, but coordination and oversight are required. Sufficient knowledge of program design, curriculum, and instruction is essential for the direction of the technical work, assessment of quality of plans and materials, and implementation.

Student services are provided through programs, and an understanding of the psychological and developmental aspects of youth is important to such services, as well as to the support and assistance schools must provide young people. Few programs are developed from the ground up. Most program planning and implementation derive from evidence obtained from program evaluations, and most entail changing established programs. Concepts and procedures needed to exercise leadership in this area come from the fields of instructional design, curriculum, and evaluation, and from psychology, human development, and learning theory.

ORGANIZATIONS AND ORGANIZATIONAL MANAGEMENT

Effective schools invariably are vital organizations, with agendas about directions of development, structures for planning and problem solving, expectations for high student and staff performance, arrangements that permit cooperative effort, and a satisfying working environment for students and staff. In an efficiently run organization, in which immediate problems are handled in a decisive and timely way, responsibilities are clearly delineated and delegated, and the protection of the time and safety of students and staff is a high priority. Along with organizational health and vitality, school leaders need to maintain open communication with individuals and groups in the school, higher authorities, and the community, as well as to arrange for necessary data gathering and appropriate information sharing. Educational leaders need knowledge of short- and long-range planning and decision making, problem analysis and action research, principles of organization and organizational leadership, knowledge of personnel evaluation and staff development, and an understanding of social systems and interpersonal relations. They need a functional knowledge of legal and fiscal requirements, technologies associated with data collection and data management, and the uses of a variety of forms of media.

GOVERNANCE AND EXTERNAL RELATIONS

Schools exist within a governance structure that determines policies and resource allocation. Principals and superintendents as leaders articulate the needs of their schools and use the governance structure as a resource rather than an impediment. To do this they need knowledge of these structures and how to influence them. They need knowledge of the processes of policy-making and of politics and how to use these processes to resolve educational issues and obtain support to deal with persistent problems. Schools are concerned with the total welfare and education of their students, and this requires knowledge of other community agencies that serve youth and how to use those agencies.

RELATED AND SUPPORTING FIELDS

As an applied field, educational administration draws concepts from many supporting fields. Management, philosophy, and the social sciences have been the traditional sources, particularly the fields of psychology, sociology, political science, and cultural anthropology. Of more recent importance are communications and computer science. Educational leaders cannot expect to master from all these fields even those ideas and concepts that are applicable to the problems of educational administration. However, they can achieve an understanding of what these fields can contribute and a level of useful competence in one or more of them. Expertise in one or more supporting fields increases educational leaders' perspective of the knowledge base and enhances their ability to make contributions to it.

CONCLUSION

Administrators become educational leaders when they are in command of the fundamental concepts that assist them in understanding the issues and problems they confront. The knowledge base provides the substance from which leaders can reach intelligent, thoughtful responses, formulate action plans, and engage with others in the resolution of persistent problems. The knowledge base of educational administration depends on the field of practice for its relevance and vitality. If schools are to succeed, principals and superintendents who are capable of a high order of competence will lead them, and they will require a knowledge base that is developed from the practice of school leadership and tested for its adequacy in practice.

REFERENCE

National Commission for the Principalship. (1990). *Principals for our changing schools: Preparation and certification.* Fairfax, VA: Author.

4. Redesigning the Preparation of School Administrators: Toward Consensus

Patrick B. Forsyth

We must begin to focus on a set of integrated propositions relating to the redesign of administrator preparation in this country.[1] Mine are stated here, without embellishment, and developed in the course of the chapter:

(1) We need to agree on the core professional tasks of school administration.

(2) Once we agree on the core professional tasks, all ways of preparing administrators are not equal, and the differences among them are important.

(3) If school administration requires certain levels of knowledge and skills, then we must select for that expertise or deliver it.

(4) A problem-based curriculum seems most appropriate for the preparation of school administrators.

(5) Utilizing a problem-based curriculum successfully will require the reorganization of theory, research, clinical history, and best practice around professional problems of practice.
(6) The reform of administrator preparation will require a radical reorganization of schools of education and the establishment of structured, permanent, relationships with schools.
(7) The intense experiences required by excellent administrator preparation, and the requisite professional socialization to collegial norms of problem finding and intervention, mandate that such preparation be a full-time endeavor.

There is virtually no common vision of what school administrators should know and be able to do. Two causes for this absence come to mind. First, the views of those in the education arm of this profession (university professors) are severely distorted by university life and its relative isolation from public schools. Second, the views of practicing administrators have been radically constrained by existing unimaginative practice and goal ambiguity. Consequently, when we speak of reforming the way school administrators and other educational professionals are prepared, both of these groups opt for the status quo, or cosmetic change, so as not to disrupt their own visions. Both groups are inexplicably perplexed by calls for radical reform; they don't know what all the fuss is about.

Because we lack a common vision, the first step in a serious reform effort depends on the formation of a set of assertions about administrator preparation that are so compelling they demand acquiescence. Let me suggest several:

(1) The core technology of education is teaching/learning.
(2) The primary role of the school administrator is problem finding and intervention with respect to teaching/learning.
(3) The purpose of preservice education of school administrators is to foster and assure knowledge and skill related to the improvement of teaching and learning.

In addition to these assertions, we should keep in mind the most important contribution of current cries for reform, that the schools be more collegial and less bureaucratic. Collegial and professional approaches to schooling are not likely to dominate the future without an explicit effort to socialize future school administrators to those values.

Given the above assertions, how should this nation prepare school administrators? The role I have outlined for them, although simply stated, is a very complex one, requiring sensitivity, intelligence, knowledge, and skill. With Etzioni, I agree that professional competence can be assured through a combination of socialization and selection.[2] Knowledge and skill that cannot be imparted, fostered, or developed must be assured through selection. All complex professions do this. People do not learn to read or reason in law school; they are admitted on condition that they can do these things. Law schools cannot teach these skills, so they must select for them. Professional preparation programs in educational administration cannot teach people to read, write, speak, or reason either. Nor can they be expected to expose candidates to fundamental democratic philosophy, national history, law, and the basics of teaching/learning that are, nonetheless, critical requirements for school administration. It is desirable that those admitted to programs preparing for careers as professional educators (teachers, counselors, administrators) should be knowledgeable, intelligent, and energetic. No one would claim that recruiting and selection to the profession should be aimed at the low ends of these continua, however they are measured, yet that may be the net effect of current self-selection procedures.

Again, I ask, how should this nation prepare school administrators? It seems reasonable that, in addition to careful selection, we should design preparation that helps people think like educators—in the case of administrators, like caretakers of teaching and learning. Learning to think like an educational administrator involves exposure to knowledge and skill, much of which is captured in the notions of problem finding and intervention. *Problem finding* does not refer to uncovering irritations. Instead, it refers to the sophisticated scanning, analysis, and reflection about people, processes, information, and systems that are relevant to teaching and learning. It means monitoring all of the factors that ultimately affect children of a particular school or district, including barriers to learning and incentives for learning. *Intervention* refers to the collaborative planning and execution of changes in the elements and conditions that affect children, learning, and the environment, especially the learning environment.

How can people be prepared to do this? We can design a successful professional program that prepares people to do sophisticated analyses of the core technology of schooling, who are informed by the theoretical and clinical evidence related to a variety of intervention strategies, and who can operate collaboratively with other school professionals. The complex professions have experimented over the years with several approaches, but the key elements in professional preparation hold rather constant. It seems reasonable that preparation for the practice of school administration should gradually give candidates authority and responsibility for problem finding and intervention in increasingly realistic settings, until an individual is licensed to practice independently.[3] The key elements adapted for school administration would include the following:

(1) the study of theory, research, and clinical writing organized around administrative problems of practice
(2) mentoring in standardized problem finding and sense making
(3) collaborative problem-finding and decision-making simulations
(4) field residency
(5) internship
(6) licensure

Each of these key elements will be discussed, some more extensively than others.

THE STUDY OF THEORY, RESEARCH, AND CLINICAL WRITING

First, let me present an analysis of the acquisition of knowledge organized around problems of practice, using a medical comparison. In premedicine, candidates for medical practice study basic physical sciences that provide them with general and abstract knowledge, and familiarity with the basic language and constructs of the physical sciences relevant to medicine. Then medical training becomes more and more oriented to clinical studies, as students move toward medical specialties. For example, cardiologists turn their attention to diagnostics, dysfunctions, health, symptoms, treatments, and the conditions under which treatments are more or less likely to work as they begin to master the specialty.

The parallel notion of a specialty in educational administration does not exist. As a profession, we have not organized what we know around diagnostics, dysfunctions, "health," symptoms, and treatments (interventions) related to teaching/learning in a school or district. Instead, our teaching and research continue to be organized around basic disciplines such as sociology, psychology, economics, law, and philosophy. Although not a perfect analogy, what we do is to send out administrative practitioners at the end of studies approximating a premedicine program. We have not collected what is known (theory, research, clinical cases, interventions) around problems of practice. There is no agreement on what the problems of administrative practice are. Again, to belabor my analogy, it is as if the profession of medicine had no agreement as to the existence of a cardiopulmonary system, did not attempt to explain its function or its relationships with other systems, conducted no organized research, did not prepare specialists, had no clinical or diagnostic traditions, and did not accumulate evidence as to the success of various treatments. Consequently, graduates of preparation programs in school administration, especially those at the doctoral level, are generally better prepared to think like fledgling social scientists than like professional school administrators.

A destructive consequence flowing from the lack of agreement on problems of practice is that there is no rationale for appropriate administrator preparation. Lacking agreement on preparation program content, the delivery system is prey to Gresham's law, providers of administrator preparation emphasizing convenience over quality. If school administration can be said to depend on a complex body of knowledge and skill directed at teaching/learning, and that its function is problem finding and intervention in a collaborative environment, and that professional competence is achieved through a gradual introduction to responsibilities in a field setting, then all delivery systems are not equal. Traditional lecture approaches seem inappropriate for much of the preparation program. Part-time, evening, or weekend approaches are questionable, because they lack the necessary scope, pervasiveness, and intensity. Such programs cannot succeed in socializing candidates to "think like professional school administrators" or coach them in necessary skills.[4] Extensive training in the methods of generalizable social science seems as superfluous to the goals of professional training for school administrators as it does for dentists. So does the writing of dissertations. Mastery of parametric statistical procedures, the conditions under which they are appropriate, interpretations of results, and so on clearly are part of the core technology used by social scientists; such skills are just as clearly not essential to the practice of school administration.

As an aside, the content of most school administration preparation programs is delivered in a piecemeal, disconnected, part-time fashion. The kind of program argued for here could not be delivered that way. The rationale for full-time, preservice, university-school-based delivery spread out over several years flows persuasively from the potentially coherent body of knowledge, skills, and socialization that I have argued is requisite for professional competence of school administrators.

What specifically is meant by "organizing knowledge, research, and practice around problems of practice"? As currently prepared, new administrators have no ways to think about their work except those they have observed others using. Empirical studies of school administrators suggest that their work is shaped by environment. For the most part, they "empty their 'in' baskets"; that is, they respond to the problems that find them. What they experienced as students of school administration is far removed from their everyday work. It is not that the theory and research they were exposed to is irrelevant, but the organization of that theory and research probably was. It was taught and studied in a way more useful to researchers than to practitioners.

An example might help make this point. Last year, the University Council on Educational Administration and the Danforth Foundation sponsored an urban initiative project, the goal of which was to distill the problems of practice in urban schools. Ten very successful urban principals were brought together for several days to help identify the focal problems of practice around which they organize their work lives. Nine such problems were identified; one was "the motivation of children to learn." Consistent with the arguments made in this chapter, to build a new knowledge base appropriate for professional school administration, the next step is to take these problems of practice and collect all that is known about them from the social sciences (theory and research), clinical records, diagnostics, and existing intervention strategies. Courses and experiences in administrator preparation programs can then be directed to these problems of practice. Researchers can begin to focus their efforts on these problems of practice and the relationships among theory, research, and intervention. A common "middle-range" professional language will emerge, one understandable to both researchers and practitioners.[5]

The example problems of practice (the motivation of children to learn) might include, for example, general motivation theories and research; social and cultural dimensions of motivation; organizational climate theories and research; research related to self-concept, locus of control, diagnostic tools, strategies, and record keeping; clinical histories of interventions; related symptoms, such as absenteeism, dropout rates, and causes—all the way to specific intervention studies such as the use of karate classes with children who have not experienced success or self-discipline in their personal or school lives. You can see from this menagerie of knowledge and activity that problems of practice, as organizing ideas, are not at all like academic disciplines, but they utilize those disciplines. They are much more likely to prove useful for teachers and administrators to focus their work in the schools. Left to the current traditions of school administration, administrators are likely to try to solve an absenteeism problem. However, socialized to their responsibility to "motivate children to learn," and having that problem of practice as a focal "way to think" about their work, school administrators are more likely to see absenteeism as a symptom of the school's failure to motivate children to learn. Solutions are more likely to evolve collaboratively with teachers, parents, and others; solutions are more likely to be long term.

This key element in administrator preparation (the study of theory, research, and clinical writing organized around problems of practice) would probably take at least a year of full-time work to complete. It would replace most or all current courses. The approach would have to be interdisciplinary, and its delivery would involve researchers, clinicians, and practitioners.

MENTORING

The second key element in administrator preparation, being mentored in standardized problem finding, also has a parallel in medical training, which utilizes the "standardized patient" as a way to mentor individual and collaborative thinking as well as diagnostic skills. Here students work alone and with small groups to find problems that have limited environments and parameters, where the conditions and possibilities are given and unchanging. Students learn to think and work with other professionals (students, faculty, practitioners) in defining problems; they learn to cope with constructive criticism, as well as to give it. They critique problem definitions of other groups and hear the problem definitions of a variety of experts. They learn not to define problems too narrowly (or too broadly) and that, even under clinical and static conditions, problem finding and definition combine art, skill, and reflection. They learn that there may not be a single best problem or problem definition, and that all efforts are not as likely to result in successful interventions.

In place of patients trained to act the same and report the same symptoms to a succession of medical students (standardized patients), case studies and case histories are the likely vehicle for this kind of work in school administration. Cases can be used to introduce students to problem finding and decision making in controlled conditions. Research and clinical professors can coach individuals and groups, fostering a collegial style of problem finding and decision making. This element serves basically as introduction to the process of administration. Although not of paramount concern at this level, the content focus should still be clearly drawn from the identified problems of practice.

COLLABORATIVE PROBLEM FINDING AND DECISION MAKING

Collaborative problem-finding and decision-making simulations, the third element mentioned above, would not be as structured as standardized problem finding. Data used for these exercises might be whole district simulations, or real districts with which permanent arrangements have been made to provide settings for these exercises (the Holmes Group's "professional development schools" might prove to be models for this kind of activity). Groups of students would immerse themselves in the simulation or district, engage in collaborative problem finding and decision making, and have their efforts examined and critiqued by colleagues, researchers, clinicians, and others. During this stage of their preparation, they would have no legal authority or responsibility in any school.

FIELD RESIDENCY

The fourth element, field residency, requires temporary administrative assignments in cooperating schools or school districts. Perhaps cooperating schools might have permanent slots to be filled by a sequence of residents. Ideally, the positions would carry with them limited authority, some responsibility, and a salary. In addition to collaboration with a field mentor, each candidate would return to the university weekly for a mandatory seminar. This seminar is analogous to the "rounds" of medical interns. In medicine, fledgling physicians visit patient bedsides as a group, discussing the cases, diagnoses, and proposed treatments. Their efforts are reviewed and questioned by fellow students and medical experts. In the educational administration seminar, students might similarly report on their problem finding and recommendations for intervention strategies. Experienced researchers, clinicians, and practitioners would also participate, offering suggestions, asking questions, proposing alternative strategies, and probing the thoroughness of the residents' analyses.

INTERNSHIP

The fifth element, internship, would take the form of a probationary period of actual practice. In this final transition to independent practice, mentoring, support, and a system of feedback should be available to interns. An intern might ultimately be employed in the district he or she interns in. It might be argued that the internship should be managed by a statewide board of professional practice. The mechanisms, the personnel, and decisions about competence to practice might be board controlled, with university representation.

LICENSURE

The last element, licensure, has been a state function for many years. The concept of state licensure, licensing procedures, and licensing policies will all have to be changed to enable the preparation approach argued here. What is necessary is enabling legislation and policy, with the state and the profession cooperating to examine professional competence after preparation is completed and before independent practice begins. The state should also work to eliminate the barriers that inhibit change to this kind of administrator preparation, and to eliminate rewards that sustain the status quo.

As Glazer (1974, p. 363) has suggested, building consensus about the requisite knowledge and skill necessary for school administrators will be difficult. However, the consequences of not moving in that direction may be the elimination of professional schools of education and the establishment of apprenticeship training for the education professions. I would suggest that the balance of art and knowledge required for school administration argues for housing administrator preparation in the university, unless the university refuses to change.

NOTES

1. This particular vision is an effort to glean compatible notions about administrator preparation from a series of studies and reports issued in the last five years. The most influential resources were works by the National Commission on Excellence in Educational Administration (1987), the National Policy Board for Educational Administration (1989, 1990), the National Association of Elementary School Principals (1990), Clifford and Guthrie (1988), Lieberman (1988), the Holmes Group (1990), Daresh and Playko (1990), Murphy (1990), and Mulkeen and Cooper (1989). I would like to express my appreciation to these authors, whose ideas have been freely borrowed and adapted.

2. For a discussion of professional recruitment versus selection, see Etzioni (1961).

3. In the last few years, for example, medical schools have increasingly moved toward the notion of problem-based curriculum. The approach is not without its drawbacks and skeptics, but it appears to be gaining strength. For a recent discussion, see the October 17, 1990, issue of the *Chronicle of Higher Education.*

4. For a discussion of pervasiveness and scope, see Etzioni (1961, pp. 264-278).

5. To bridge practice and research successfully, the problems of practice must be relatively few in number (under 10) and must be stated at a middle-range level of abstraction. They must be concrete enough to serve as actual foci for the work of school administrators; they must be abstract enough so they are of interest to researchers. They cannot be directed to administrative and bureaucratic skills (such as "scheduling") that must be learned on the job, because these are idiosyncratic to schools and school systems.

REFERENCES

Clifford, G. J., & Guthrie, J. W. (1988). *Ed school.* Chicago: University of Chicago Press.

Daresh, J. C., & Playko, M. A. (1990). *Preservice administrative mentoring: Reflections of the mentors.* Paper presented at the annual meeting of the American Educational Research Association, Boston.

Etzioni, A. (1961). *A comparative analysis of complex organizations.* New York: Free Press.

Glazer, N. (1974). The schools of the minor professions. *Minerva, 12*(3).

Holmes Group. (1990). *Tomorrow's schools: Principles for the design of professional development schools.* East Lansing, MI: Author.

Lieberman, A. (1988). *Building a professional culture in schools.* New York: Teachers College Press.

Mulkeen, T. R., & Cooper, B. S. (1989). *Implications of preparing school administrators for knowledge-work organizations.* Paper presented at the annual meeting of the American Educational Research Association, San Francisco.

Murphy, J. (1990). Restructuring the technical core of preparation programs in educational administration. *UCEA Review, 31*(3).

National Association of Elementary School Principals. (1990). *Principals for 21st century schools.* Alexandria, VA: Author.

National Commission on Excellence in Educational Administration. (1987). *Leaders for America's schools: The report of the National Commission on Excellence in Educational Administration.* University Park, PA: University Council on Educational Administration.

National Policy Board for Educational Administration. (1989). *Improving the preparation of school administrators: An agenda for reform.* Fairfax, VA: Author.

National Policy Board for Educational Administration. (1990). *The preparation of school administrators.* Fairfax, VA: Author.

5. Professional Certification and Licensure: Governance, Organization, and Procedures

B. Dean Bowles

National certification and state licensure should be separate and should serve different objectives. States should continue to license educational professionals and establish standards for university preparation program approval. States have traditionally performed these tasks by (a) establishing minimal criteria and standards, (b) assuring a supply of licensed professionals, (c) terminating licenses for malfeasance and gross incompetence, (d) regulating program approval standards, and (e) brokering conflict among political interests surrounding supply-demand, labor-management, public-private, and university-profession issues. These are appropriate and necessary functions, but ones that should not be shouldered by national certification.

GOAL OF NATIONAL CERTIFICATION

By contrast, national professional certification should establish goals, criteria, and standards for professional certification and institutional accreditation that are based on the principle of *excellence.* National certification will *not* be able to act on the principle of excellence if it becomes entangled with functions of minimums, labor supply, license termination, regulation, and political brokering. Nor should national certification become engulfed in the sovereign traditions of 50 state political cultures.

However, this is not to suggest that national certification and state licensure are incompatible. They are compatible. National certification should (a) act independently to certify individuals and approve preparation programs, (b) cooperate to raise state minimum standards for licensure and preparation program approval, (c) seek automatic interstate licensure for professionals and preparation program approval through national certification and institutional accreditation standards, and (d) achieve national certification as an alternative route to state licensure. National certification and institutional accreditation should neither seek a state role nor impose its standards on the states, but should become a beacon of excellence through rigorous and high standards.

NATIONAL STRATEGY

If a national certification board assesses tasks and then develops a national consensus for school administration generally and each position specifically, the result will be a significant national influence on preparation programs and licensure practices in the states. Similarly, each of the 8 design criteria and 11 requirements for national certification discussed below should be seen not only as operational tasks of a national board but also as means to influence state political leaders, state educational agencies, state and local professional associations, and university preparation programs.

If the notion of national certification and institutional accreditation achieves the dual goals of excellence and credibility, it will become a significant national influence. However, it will do so only if the national board avoids direct confrontation with the states and maintains the moral high ground of excellence.

GOVERNING AND MANAGING NATIONAL CERTIFICATION

National certification should be governed by a national board of standards for educational administration. This board should be composed of the following representatives:

- colleges and universities that prepare school administrators, including representatives from research institutions, land-grant universities, state colleges, and independent colleges and universities
- national university professional associations
- national university accrediting groups
- national, state, and local school administrators' associations and superintendents, principals, school business officials, and directors of curriculum, special education, and pupil services
- national teachers' associations and unions
- national school board associations
- state school board associations
- chief state school officers
- state certification and licensing officials
- the Education Commission of the States
- urban school administrators
- women and minorities

The powers of the national board would include (a) appointing an executive director; (b) approving an annual budget; (c) establishing criteria, standards, and processes for national certification and institutional accreditation; (d) approving assessment criteria, standards, and processes, including national professional examinations of knowledge and skills; (e) appointing and supervising state and local review panels for certification and accreditation; (f) maintaining effective government and public relations and promotion of the board's goals; and (g) commissioning policy and evaluation research necessary to its mission. The national board would hire an executive director, who in turn would appoint a small professional staff.

The national board should rely on grants for development and research projects, and on fees for the direct costs of processing national certification and administering institutional accreditations. The costs of improving preparation programs would rest with universities, state educational agencies, or local school districts through general fund or categorical aid programs. The work of the national board should not rely heavily on fees, because the need for revenue would compromise the goal of excellence.

RELATION OF INSTITUTIONAL ACCREDITATION TO NATIONAL CERTIFICATION

National certification should be the primary purpose of the national board, but institutional accreditation should become the principal means to the end of certification. For all practical purposes, this means that prospective administrators should be able to achieve national certification whether or not they attended an institution accredited by the national board. However, there are good reasons to proceed with institutional accreditation. First, a program of institutional accreditation should improve the preparation of all prospective administrators. Second, institutional accreditation should encourage new administrators to seek national certification. Third, institutional accreditation should work to upgrade the standards of state program approval and independent accreditation agencies. Fourth, institutional accreditation should encourage a system of state reciprocity for administrative licenses. Fifth, institutional accreditation should reduce the administration and program costs of national certification. In summary, the national board should assure that institutional accreditation does not supplant either state program approval or independent accreditation by other agencies. Rather, the aim would be to leverage those efforts with the standards of excellence established by the national board and to seek an integration of purpose, criteria, standard, and process over time.

DESIGN CRITERIA

The design criteria of a program of national certification should be based on the following eight principles:

(1) *Assessment and consensus.* A periodical assessment and identification of the leadership responsibilities and management tasks should lead to a consensus about which should be part of a program of national certification of school administrators.

(2) *Admission.* Standards of admission to university preparation programs ought to identify the best and brightest, require experience and excellence in teaching, provide evidence of successful leadership, assess leadership skills, assure equity for women and minorities, and select for qualities that cannot be learned or trained.

(3) *Knowledge, skills, and practice.* The identified leadership and management needs should be transformed into a curriculum of both common and specific knowledge and skills that are organized around problems and issues of practice.

(4) *Professional practice and improvement.* Certification should be achieved through professional practice and improvement that encourages the application of knowledge and skills in a program of systematic, monitored, and successively responsible professional practice based on Deming's notions of continuous quality improvement.

(5) Outcomes and performance standards. A national certification and accreditation program should be based on outcomes and performance standards, including appropriate and multiple assessments of leadership and management knowledge, skills, and applications to a variety of problems and contexts.

(6) *Levels of certification.* Two levels of achievement should be established: provisional and national.

(7) *Renewal.* Renewal of national certification and institutional accreditation should be required on a periodic basis, based on Deming's notion of continuous quality improvement.

(8) *Alternative certification.* A national certification program should provide for alternative certification that does not (a) discourage professionals from seeking national certification, (b) undermine the development of institutional accreditation of quality university preparation programs, (c) abandon state initiatives for quality improvement, or (d) compromise standards of practice.

If the National Board is to achieve its goal, each of the above design elements should be addressed, integrated, and specified in sufficient detail so that it will constitute a measurable criteria and standard against which to evaluate applications for certification and accreditation.

PROVISIONAL CERTIFICATION

The content, competencies, and performances that should be evaluated and the requirements for provisional certification are set forth below.

(1) *Preparation program.* Admission to a university preparation program (preferably accredited) with a grade point average and test scores that are equivalent to those in comparable professional fields should be the first requirement.

(2) *Teaching experience.* At least three years' teaching experience should be required, with demonstrated excellence based on several common competency and performance criteria and standards.

(3) *Leadership potential.* Successful leadership experience or potential in school or community affairs should be demonstrated and evaluated through common criteria and standards.

(4) *Assessment center.* Those seeking provisional certification should complete an assessment center program that addresses leadership responsibilities, management tasks, and administrator behaviors of school administrators and that is approved by the national board. The results should be submitted to university preparation programs so that programs can be developed that address weaknesses and enhance strengths.

(5) *Character.* Applicants for provisional certification should undergo exhaustive reference checks and personal interviews to determine administrative competence, personal leadership qualities, and moral character. Reference checks and interviews should be collaborative efforts between faculty of university preparation programs and school administrators.

(6) *Degree.* Provisional certification should require completion of an appropriate graduate degree, which may include a two-year master's degree or other certificate.

(7) *Knowledge and skills.* Provisional certification should provide a program and curriculum that assures knowledge, skills, and application (where appropriate) in each of the following areas of study:

- interpersonal and communications skills, including speaking, writing, listening, observation, group process, and conflict-resolution skills
- inquiry skills, including problem framing, conceptualization, analysis and synthesis, and operations, marketing, and policy research
- teaching and learning, including curriculum development and program assessment

- child, early adolescent, and adolescent development, learning, and psychology
- the historical, social, political, economic, demographic, legal, and governmental context of schooling
- leadership and management, including organizational theory, personnel administration, budgeting, planning, evaluation, and other operational tasks specific to particular positions

These sets of knowledge and skills are based on an exhaustive review of literature, earlier proposals by the National Policy Board for Educational Administration, an examination of the Danforth Project initiatives, competencies from assessment center exercises, proposals by the National Commission on the Principalship, and the proposals incorporated in the Wisconsin *Report on Leadership, Training, and Licensure.* There are others of similar or comparable scope and detail. The point is that the national board should (a) identify the knowledge and skills that are useful to understanding and dealing with problems of administrative practice, (b) establish priorities among competing curriculum values, (c) sort the knowledge and skills into general knowledge and skills for all administration and specific knowledge and skills for a position, (d) establish a common core and specific curricula, (e) provide for assessment of each area of knowledge and skill through a practice-driven, performance-based system, and (f) seek and establish a consensus on both the curriculum and assessment system.

(8) *Examination.* Provisional certification should require an examination on knowledge and skills associated with education, leadership, management, and educational administration specifically. This examination should be approved by the national board.

(9) *Application of knowledge and skills.* Provisional certification should demand evidence of application of knowledge and skills to real and simulated administrative problems of practice. The simulated experiences may include opportunities for reflective practice, portfolios of leadership activities, case studies, simulations, evaluated field experiences, and assessment centers.

(10) *Internship.* Completion of a one-year, full-time paid internship, including participation in a mentor program and a university classroom component with other interns and practitioners, should be required for provisional certification.

(11) *National board panel.* A favorable review by a national board panel should be required before provisional certification may be granted by the national board.

NATIONAL CERTIFICATION

The content, competencies, and performances that should be evaluated (following a minimum of five years of successful, full-time administrative experience) and the requirements for national certification are set forth below.

(1) *Demonstrated leadership.* National certification should require evidence of demonstrated, successful leadership and management in school administration.

(2) *Degree.* National certification should provide for the completion of an appropriate second or terminal graduate degree.

(3) *Knowledge and skills.* National certification should provide a program and curriculum that assures advanced knowledge, skills, and application (where appropriate) in each of the following areas of study:
- teaching and learning, including curriculum development and program assessment
- child, early adolescent, and adolescent development, learning, and psychology
- the historical, social, political, economic, demographic, legal, and governmental context of schooling
- leadership and management, including organizational theory, personnel administration, budgeting, planning, evaluation, and other operational tasks specific to particular positions

(4) *Application of knowledge and skills.* National certification should demand evidence of continued, successful application of knowledge and skills to real and simulated administrative problems of practice.

(5) *Mentor program.* Participation in a mentor program with a university classroom component with other practitioners should be required for national certification.

(6) *Examination.* National certification should require passing an *advanced* examination on knowledge and skills associated with education, leadership, management, and educational administration specifically. This examination should be approved by the national board.

(7) *National board panel.* A favorable review by a national board panel should be required before national certification may be granted by the national board. Review by a national board panel may grant national certification valid for five years.

ASSESSMENT INSTRUMENTS AND PROCESSES

Principles

Several principles of assessment should guide a national certification board. The first is that assessment should be performance based, with observable and measurable outcomes. The second principle should be that assessment ought primarily to be formative, with summative assessments largely reserved to final decisions on admission to preparation programs, internships, and certification. A third principle is that the spirit of assessment should capture Deming's concept of continuous quality improvement. Fourth, assessments and passing scores on examinations should be governed by national board-approved standards and not norm references. Fifth, assessment should encourage reflective rather than reflexive practice. Finally, the assessment program should make frequent assessments based on multiple sources of quantitative and qualitative information.

Instruments

Among instruments that should be utilized in the national board's assessment program include assessment centers, observed and evaluated case studies and simulations, portfolios of leadership and management experiences, evaluated field experiences, experiences that offer opportunities for evaluated reflective practice, demonstrations of application of knowledge and skill in an administrative context or to problems of practice, and national board-approved examinations.

Processes

The following processes should be employed at appropriate places in the certification process. However, performance criteria, standards, and processes should be established by the national board.

(1) Faculty at preparation institutions should be responsible for admission to preparation programs in collaboration with practitioners, who

should recommend candidates, serve as references, and participate on interview panels.

(2) Faculty in preparation programs should establish performance criteria and standards for all knowledge and skills included in the curriculum, such as providing opportunities for case studies, simulations, reflective practice, and demonstrations and applications of knowledge and skills. In short, not only should the traditional curriculum change, but also the teaching style and methods of assessment.

(3) Faculty in preparation programs should evaluate field experiences and the internship in collaboration with the supervising administrator.

(4) Professional associations, preparation programs, and state educational agencies should operate assessment centers that report the results to the participant and the preparation program.

(5) Mentor programs should be collaborations between preparation programs and practitioners in which field experiences and problems of practice are examined and simulated performance evaluated.

(6) The national board should approve the criteria, standards, form, and procedure for the two national examinations of knowledge and skills.

National Board Review Panels

Finally, national board review panels should evaluate candidates for provisional and national certification and any recertification process. These review panels should be composed of the following four representatives:

- an administrator who supervises and evaluates the candidate in the district of employment
- a national board-appointed faculty member from an accredited preparation program
- a national board-appointed practitioner administrator from another district in the state
- a national board-appointed practitioner from another state, who would chair the review panel

These review panels would review and recommend for certification to the national board all persons seeking provisional certification, national certification, or recertification. They would not recommend or become entangled in state licensure decisions or employment retention actions.

For provisional or national certification, the review panel would (a) examine all the evidence, including the internship and employment evaluations, portfolios, and examination results; (b) make a formative evaluation that includes a plan for continuous quality improvement for the next five years in conjunction with the representatives of the preparation program and employing school district; and (c) render a summary evaluation on the qualifications of the candidate for certification, including a recommendation to the national board. The review panel could recommend against initial certification, continuation of provisional certification, or decertification. An appeal of a negative action would be reviewed by a second review panel appointed by the national board, and then by the board itself.

EQUITY SAFEGUARDS

Affirmative action policies, preparation program modifications, and national board criteria, standards, and processes must continually be monitored to assure the following:

(1) Admissions to preparation programs leading to national certification provide opportunities for women and minorities that are consistent with their proportion in the population in the state and region served by a preparation program.
(2) Preparation programs make program modifications so that the retention of women and minorities achieves the twin goals of quantity and quality.
(3) Effective affirmative action programs have goals, measurable outcomes, and action plans.
(4) Different programs, policies, and practices are explored if needed to meet the needs of each group affected by affirmative action goals.
(5) Assessment criteria, standards, and processes, including examinations, are judged to avoid both stereotyping and bias.
(6) Barriers to professional employment are eliminated—such action may include expanding the national board's role to include recommending employment practices, job security arrangements, and administrator-board relationships for states and local school districts.

In summary, the national board should establish criteria and standards to assure equity and promote model programs to facilitate affirmative action in states and universities. Considerable lip service has been given to the questions of equity for women and minorities in school administration. The national board should assume the added responsibility of addressing these issues outside the narrower framework of stereotyping and bias.

WHOM TO CERTIFY FIRST?

The administrative positions that should be certified first are those directly associated with the central mission of the school: principals, superintendents, and directors of curriculum and instruction. However, the national board should focus its current resources on developing, piloting, and implementing certification criteria, standards, and processes for the position of principal.

6. Strengthening Professionalism: The Ethical Dimensions

Michael P. Thomas

The Code of Hammurabi states, "If a builder builds a house for a man and does not make its construction firm, and the house which he has built collapses and causes the death of the owner's son, they shall put to death a son of that builder." This stern warning about professional conduct and ethics is one that, if nothing else, must have ensured that builders' sons took a lively interest in their fathers' performance standards.[1] Professionalism and performance standards seem to go hand in hand, and they are inseparable from a concept of ethics. If one were to complicate the issue by proposing performance standards for programs that prepare builders, with suitable assertive disciplines, there would be a fine parallel to the problem of maintaining professional standards in educational administration.

STANDARDS AND PROFESSIONAL PREPARATION PROGRAMS

Modeling professional standards should begin with professional preparation programs, which should be held to the highest ethical demands wherever they are lodged. Those ethical standards should address at least two issues: (a) the selection of people who on some basis it might be predicted have the potential for high-level performance in the administration of America's schools, and (b) the character of the programs themselves and the resources available for their prosecution.

A profession takes its character from the nature of the enterprise—building from engineering, medicine from curing (or preventing) illness, and so on. Schools have to do with learning and with enculturating, specifically, in the United States, for preparing students to function in a political democracy. It would seem that if an individual is to lead an enterprise devoted to learning, he or she should be learned. That is, he or she should understand the rules for carrying on intelligent discourse about serious issues facing the great American experiment in free public education for all the nation's children. If a person is to lead an enterprise devoted to preserving and enhancing the culture, he or she should understand that culture, its history, and its prospects. Professional educational leadership demands at least those two attributes in a person if he or she is to serve as a model of the educated individual. The National Policy Board for Educational Administration should use its own moral force to encourage programs to select candidates for the leadership of institutions devoted to learning who are themselves learners and who have a sense for the business of producing knowledge.

Honesty in Packaging

Preparation programs for professionals should be held to a strict standard of honesty in their claims for what they can offer prospective students; these claims may vary among programs, and may not bear a relationship to what it is that students do upon completing a program. At its simplest, if a program is designed to prepare people to do research to add to the knowledge base in one of the traditional areas of inquiry of our field, then it should be clear about that, and its courses, faculty, and other resources should be sufficient to the task. If a program is designed to prepare practitioners at the highest level, then its resources should be sufficient to that task. It is important from an ethical point of view that programs lay claim only to what they have the resources to deliver. One might think of this principle as honesty in packaging. Claims to professionalism in professional preparation are diminished by anything less. The Policy Board has a responsibility to monitor preparation programs on the basis of their claims for performance. The model of regional accrediting agencies might be a good one, based as they are on an assessment procedure that evaluates programs on the basis of their own objectives.

LEADERSHIP FOR THE COMMON GOOD

Standards for professional performance of leaders in organizations devoted to the commonweal should be unusually rigorous, inasmuch as those organizations perform functions that are central to the well-being of civil life. It is the character of schools as commonweal organizations, rather than specifics such as compulsory attendance, that sets schools apart from other types of organizations. Professional standards that should be key to administrators in schools include the following:

(1) a keen sense of distributive justice, especially as it comes to bear in discussions of equity and access to educational opportunity

(2) a commitment to acting on the belief that all individuals are ends and should never be used as means to an end, a belief that is consistent with traditions of individualized education and objectives of helping each child reach his or her potential (I have chosen these Kantian principles because Kant, among all the philosophers, seems most committed to protecting the individual as an autonomous moral agent, and to the principles of individual freedom and worth that have been part of the rhetoric of education in the United States for decades.)

(3) a willingness to act on the basis of justice and fairness

(4) a commitment to informing decisions with knowledge of the best available research and the traditions of thought about issues related to those decisions

At the very least, the National Policy Board for Educational Administration should constitute a forum to reach some agreement about ethical principles for the public administration of institutions devoted to learning. At best, the Board, together with its constituent components, should promulgate a few simple, powerful statements that clearly center the role of school administrators in promoting the common good.

THE PUBLIC INTEREST

Maintaining a vital, alert, and competent profession probably cannot be accomplished simply through accreditation and certification. The experience of regional accrediting agencies should be informative here. A structure must be designed, through the auspices of the Policy Board, that can capitalize on the talents of all who are involved in the study and practice of school administration; the Board should provide occasions for serious discussion and debate about the prevailing issues facing education in the United States and for speaking out against conditions that are antithetical to the conduct of schools guided by the ethical principles proposed above. A "national college of educational leadership"—not a place, but a concept—could serve to bring together leaders to address those conditions. Professionalism is not strengthened by workshops devoted to style or technique alone. Indeed, we may be in danger of substituting technique for substance in both our preparation programs and subsequent professional development. A healthy profession should be able to draw on its knowledge base, its traditions, and its collective understanding of what is right to proclaim its sense of what constitutes the fair, equitable, just, and warranted conditions for administering effective schools. A national college of educational leadership could assemble the talent of our profession to shape such proclamations when they are needed.

On the issue of the role of professionals vis-à-vis the electorate, it would follow from some of the ideas proposed above that the profession should be in the forefront in informing the electorate of what the conditions for effective learning are, and in securing the resources to obtain those conditions. Our political responsibilities are not met by accommodating without protest to conditions that make effective schooling impossible. Although we must recognize that the definition of the common good is the responsibility of the body politic, I believe we must avoid bargaining when it comes to those practices and policies that, as a profession, we know are necessary to fair, equitable, and informed schooling.

At this time, in most places, the preparation of each of the variety of educational professionals who combine their efforts in schools is done virtually in isolation. Teacher education programs, counselor programs, school psychology programs, programs for instructional supervisors—all are conducted without reference to what is going on in the others. There are certainly points of intersection where future teachers and administrators in preparation should be involved in common educational experiences and common discussions. That these experiences and discussions do not occur is generally the fault of the structure of colleges of education, which promotes ownership of programs. It is doubtful that faculty members in one program fully understand the values and practices promoted by another program. The Policy Board should consider initiating discussions that might result in some number of colleges of education becoming laboratories for designing programs for the education profession, and should provide leadership in the design of such programs. At some point, teacher organizations and organizations representing other educational professionals must be involved to identify those experiences that should be common to all. Integrating the preparation programs of education professionals would, then, be the starting point for integrating the preparation of other professional groups, such as social workers, more directly with the schools.

NOTE

1. Excerpted from a speech by Professor John Breen, College of Engineering, The University of Texas, Austin.

Index

Accreditation, 37, 42, 43
American Medical International, 5
Assessment, 10, 11
  board-certified, 42
  center, 39
  data analysis, 11

Bolman, Lee G., 3, 4

Certification, 34-41
  board, 35, 36, 41
  national, 35-37, 40-42
  provisional, 39, 40
  review panels, 43
  state, 34-36
Change
  obstacles to, 2, 24, 50
  process, 25
Clinical experience, 26, 27, 29, 30, 31, 40, 42
  field residency, 31
  internship, 26, 31
Collaboration, 26, 27, 30, 50
Curriculum
  problem based, 23, 24, 27, 28, 29, 30

Danforth Foundation, 28, 40
Decision making, 30, 50
Delegation, 20
Demographics, 8, 9

Education
  financing, 13
  program, 20
Equity, 44, 48
Ethics, 19, 48
Expectations, public, 9, 10, 12, 13

Governance, 21

Human resource
  group dynamics, 5
  interpersonal, 5, 50
  leadership, 3, 4, 25

Knowledge base, 16-18, 19-22, 24, 26, 27, 29, 38, 39, 41, 48
Kotter, J.P., 5

Leadership
  communication, 10, 11, 12, 19, 20
  cultural, 3, 4, 9, 19, 20, 47

definitions of, 2, 3, 29
educational, 8, 9, 10, 12, 19, 20, 24, 25, 29, 50
experience, 5, 6, 18, 39, 41
innovations, 6, 8
management, 2, 5, 7, 20, 21
political, 3, 4, 9, 12, 17, 19, 21, 47, 48, 49
schooling, 8, 10, 29
structural, 3, 4
symbolic, 3, 4, 10, 21
Licensure, 32, 34-36

Mentoring, 26, 28, 30, 41, 43
Motivation, 17

National Center for Education Leadership, 2
National Commission for the Principalship, 2, 18, 40
National Policy Board for Educational Administration, 19, 40, 47, 48, 49

Performance standards, 38, 46, 47
Planning, 20
Practice, 18, 24, 26, 29
Preparation programs, 8, 14, 23-32, 39, 40, 42, 47, 50
Problem finding, 25, 26
Professionalism, 49

Research, 18

School reorganization, 24, 50
Selection, 25, 38, 44
Socialization, 25, 47
Social sciences, 21, 27, 29, 40
Social services, 12
Staff development, 11, 21
Student achievement, 8, 9, 10, 28, 48
Student services, 20

Tasks, 23
Teachers, 11, 50
employee relations, 14
performance, 20
Theory, 26

University Council on Educational Administration, 28

Values, 17, 19, 39, 47, 48
Vision, 15, 19, 24

Work force, 12